Get a Job Fast

The Single Best Resource Available to Help You Land Your Dream Job

---

Scott Schwefel

Published by GetaJobFast.com

Copyright, 2011

ISBN 978-0-578-07681-2

Edited by Scottie Nicole Schwefel

Table of Contents

Introduction

1. Discover Your Passion
2. Defining Career Success
3. Your Personality Style
4. Setting Goals
5. Learning to Think!

    The Power of our Minds

    Programming your Mind

    Visual, Auditory and Kinesthetic Learners

6. Integrity
7. Execution
8. Giving Back

Conclusion

Introduction

This book starts with a promise. Read it and answer the questions thoughtfully, and you will get a job fast. If you do not get the job you want after finishing this book, completing the exercises, and spending 90 days to make it happen, then return your copy with the completed exercises to us, and your proof of purchase, and we will refund your purchase price 100%.

Have you ever been given a promise like this before? It is the promise of success, if you do the work, and only 1% of you will buy this book and actually complete the exercises, even though your success is guaranteed! If you are in that committed 1%, (and I believe that you are) then let's get started.

This book is titled *Get a Job Fast*, but don't be misled by the speed of this process; ironically, getting a job fast requires some time invested upfront, but not as much as you might think. If you invest the time in thinking and planning your ideal job, ideal employer, and targeted search, you will be armed with the passion, skills, and knowledge that hiring managers (or even customers if you create your own job rather than take an existing job) will recognize. By following the steps outlined in this book, you will begin moving your career in the direction of your goals, and attaining greater happiness, job fulfillment, and financial rewards. Got a pen? Good, let's go.

Most of you probably don't have any idea of what your ideal job is. Maybe you have never even written down your career goals and aspirations. Not a problem. Using this guidebook, you will begin to discover what your God-given talents are, how to translate your talents into goals, and how to engage a time-tested success formula that dates back thousands of years in order to define and attain the job that you are most suited for, and that is valuable in today's rapidly emerging job market. You really can land the perfect job, rather than just getting any job, and realize all your dreams and career ambitions, enabling you to give back to the world more than you ever thought you could.

There are eight steps in the process for you to get a job fast. Some of you can get through them in a day, and for some others it may take weeks, or even months. If you have never really thought about your life as having mission and purpose, it will take you longer. No matter where you are at in terms of career self awareness, and whether or not you know your true purpose in life, these eight steps will prove invaluable in your search for a better career and a better you: Let's take a closer look at those 8 steps now.

Step 1. Find Your Passion – What would you do if you had all the money and all the time in the world? What parts of your previous jobs and your current life are consistent with your passion?

Step 2. Define success – in the only terms that matter, yours.

Step 3. Know your personality style, and use this knowledge to achieve your goals, and get the right job suited for your unique type.

Step 4. Set Goals – Set SMART goals around every area of your life, and write them down. Create goals for the following:
- Physical
- Spiritual
- Family
- Friends
- Financial/Work

Step 5. Think! – Engage your wonderful, powerful portable super computer brain. Post your goals, and read them daily. Your defined and positive thoughts will begin to shape your daily actions, which in turn, will lead to your inevitably successful future.

Step 6. Operate with Integrity – Know that your personal and professional life are intertwined and that you cannot live these two aspects of your life separately. Choose to operate both with character and surround yourself with people and professional endeavors that aim to do the same. Know that every word you speak has an impact on your life and plan to spend your time in ways that have a positive impact on yourself and others.

Step 7. Execute – Lay out a plan that helps move you towards your goals. Remember that your passion and goals will sustain you through the hard times, and understand that failure and quitting are NOT options. Execution is not the hardest part of this program, knowing WHAT to execute on, is.

Step 8. Give back – Success, when measured by what you alone achieve will never sustain you long term, nor will it enable you to give back. Start now by giving out a smile when you can, a helping hand, and realize you are planting the seeds of giving in your life which will enable you to look back on a long life, and feel it was well lived. We all have something to give, no matter what our present circumstances.

Will thoughtfully walking through these eight steps help you get a job fast? Yes. I say this from my own personal experience, and also because I have heard back from hundreds of others who have been through this program that it worked for them too.

I am living proof that the formula works, because I used it to get a job, and then later buy and build up that business and sell it for more than a million dollars in 2003. During the 15 years it took me to accomplish this, I interviewed literally hundreds of prospective employees, and of the nearly 500 people I interviewed, no more than five understood the principles in this book well enough to make me realize (within minutes) that they were the type of people I would absolutely hire.

What made me so certain that these interviewees were indispensible? What did they have that the other hundreds who were undoubtedly well-educated and professionally qualified for the job at hand lacked? It was the fact that this small handful of job hopefuls had done their research on my company, and also on all my competitors. They had researched the industry we were in (technology training and consulting) and they knew, without question, that their acquired skills were perfect for the position we had advertised. Most importantly, they had done the personal work in advance to **confirm** for themselves that their skills, passions and attitudes were clearly aligned with the position they were seeking, the company that offered the position, and the industry in which we were in. They were unstoppable; equipped with an attitude that cannot be featured on a resume in twelve point font. These prospective employees were indispensible because they embodied the kind of self-confidence that only hard work, passion, and honesty provides.

Were you unstoppable, secure and confident, the last time you interviewed for a job? Complete the exercises in this book, and the next time you interview you will be.

The pre-work that these successful candidates did (that undoubtedly secured them a position at my firm) doesn't sound so difficult. So why had all the others (over 99% percent of the hopefuls I interviewed over twenty years) failed to do the same?

Because no one ever told them, or showed them how to do it. Pure and simple.

I urge you, be that one percent. Understand, acquire, and use the tools you will learn through reading this book to make yourself not only indispensible in the career of your dreams, but to foster an internal peace and fulfillment that only success bred of passion can bring.

That is why I have created this guidebook, this how- to manual; to share the time-tested formula for empowering job search skills and career success with others, and to walk you through the same steps which will help you achieve your own career goals, and get a job fast. But not just *a* job; *the right job*, in the *right* company in the *right* industry- based on your unique passions and skills. This job search formula definitely works, it's been proven millions of times, and you and you alone can determine its effectiveness in getting a job fast. *The right job*, in the *right* company in the *right* industry.

Your job search success will be based upon your commitment to doing the work, and staying the course. They don't call them adages without reason; you reap what you sow, the early bird gets the worm, you make your bed etc. These are time tested equations for success that will never change. It is just as hard to be looking for work, or working in a dead end job, doing work that you don't enjoy your entire life, as it is to do work that you love, making tons of money, while giving back to your friends and your community. In fact, it is actually EASIER to do the latter, but most of us have simply never had the roadmap laid out for us.

This guidebook shows you that there actually is a roadmap to success and self-confidence, and that you are the next person that will again show that anyone can put these principles into place, stay the course, and deliver the results that you want, in a systematic way, and that nothing can stop you from reaching the pinnacle of success for which you are destined. This formula not only works to help you get a job fast, it will also work for you whether your goal is to be a better father, a more loving and caring wife, a successful entrepreneur, or a kindergarten teacher out to change the world.

Please take the time to complete the exercises in this guidebook, even if you are unsure of yourself and your true passion in life. I am convinced that if you stay the course, and complete this guidebook, that you will realize all your dreams, and live the successful life you wish for, using your unique talents to be both a success and to make the world a better place to live.

If you are truly committed, and passionate about reaching your potential, and living a life that matters, please email me with your comments, and more specifically, with the career goals that you develop as a result of using this guidebook, and I will personally support you in any way that I can.

God bless, and here's to your success.

Scott

scott@getajobfast.com

Step 1 2 3 4 5 6 7 8

Discover Your Passion

If there is one common characteristic among successful people that I have seen in my last twenty years as a businessperson, it is that they have passion for what they do. The definitions of these words however; have become muddy in the modern world. More often than not, "success" is measured in capital, and the word "passion" is extracted from the formula entirely. I cannot stress how important it is to detach yourself from this assumption (that money = success), because I don't care how shiny your stuff is, or how big your house is - if you don't have passion, you don't have anything. From here on out, when you hear the word "success" I want you to think of it in terms of fulfillment earned through passion, in doing what you love, personal integrity in everything you do, and your ability to give back to a worthy cause.

For most *truly* successful people, whether they are homemakers, CEOs, or athletes, there is a genuine "love of the game" that they all share. What are you passionate about? When was the last time you even thought about your passion?

Two of my passions have always been learning, and technology. I enjoy teaching and learning, and I have always sought out the latest and greatest technology gadgets that I could find. It is no surprise that I spent a dozen years, and made my mark in running and owning a technology training company. The company I founded, Benchmark Learning, is now the largest computer technology training firm in Minnesota. I succeeded in large part because I was doing work I loved. Do you love the work that you do, or do you, like millions of people, enter your work week with a growing sense of apprehension Sunday night, about 6pm, as you settle down, and realize that the weekend is almost over, and that you are now confronted with yet another Monday, another day at the office, slaving away for your precious salary, a salary that barely pays your bills month to month? Are you eager to make it to "hump day", and then looking ahead yet again to Friday? What a sad declaration about how we as adults relish in the "TGIF" mentality. Thank-God-it's-Friday is the saddest statement anyone could make about the occupations we have; the work that we do. The playwright Noel Coward once said, "Work is more fun than fun". Is this true for you? When was it last true for you? Ever?

When we were children, we thought about our futures with excitement. We were adventurous; we climbed trees solely because they were high and proudly wore the scrapes on our knees as medals of honor. The term "success" was rarely in our young vocabularies, but in our hearts we knew. We understood that time at the batting cage meant more hits in the game, and that hours mixing the right amount of baking soda and vinegar meant one mean science-fair volcano; we had passion simply because we were having fun. In answer to the question often asked of us by adults, "What do you want to be when you grow up?" We were able to answer in an instant, "Fireman" "Teacher" "Professional Baseball Player". One of the most successful television commercials of all time was the Monster.com black and white ad that aired during Super Bowl XXXI. Remember the one, featuring young kids, (my daughter, McKenzie was one of them) reflecting on what they wanted to be when they grow up. It struck a chord with literally millions of adults, who had forgotten their long lost dreams of what they all wanted to be when they grew up, and how truly miserable so many of us are in our jobs today. Why is this the case? When did it all go so wrong? Unfortunately, not many of us have the time (or flying capabilities) to wait at our window sill for Peter Pan to come take our hands and remind us of what we once wanted to be. So remember right here, right now (sans fairy dust).

1. Write down what you always wanted to be when you grew up.

_____

Here's a hint, can't remember? Call your mother, she does.

Note – Since you have already read this far, ONLY continue with this program if you are committed to thinking about the questions, <u>and thoughtfully writing down your answers</u>. To put it simply, the winners among you will complete the exercises, and reap the rewards. Remember that only one percent of you will complete all these exercises, so decide right now, it's as easy as grabbing a pen, and filling in the blanks. Are you in the 1%, committed to success, or are you bringing up the rear with the other 99%? Change your life, reach your dreams, live with passion, get a pen now and start writing. You are worthy of the 1%, you deserve it.

2. What was it about your childhood dream that captured your imagination? What could you not wait to do after sprinting from the bus stop and setting down your backpack?

_____
_____
_____
_____

3. What unique skills and talents did/do you possess that made you ideally want to do this when you grew up?

_____
_____
_____
_____

Why was it so exciting for you to do?

_____

_____

_____

_____

4. What do you do today, or what was the last job you had?

_____

_____

_____

_____

5. What aspects of what you do now (or did) if any, are similar to your childhood dream?

_____

_____

_____

_____

6. Are you in the right job today, or was the last job you had just right for you.

Yes, or No? Why, what was missing?

_____

_____

_____

_____

I am not suggesting that we all hate our jobs, but how many of us truly *love* the work that we do. Do you? Did you? Would you do it if you weren't paid to show up at work? I used to have a plaque on my office wall that said, "TGIM", or Thank God it's Monday! How many of us would hang the same plaque up, and believe it? Would any of us even show up to work if we didn't get paid?

It's troubling that millions of people leave their hearts and their spirit at home, reserved for the weekend, or for their after work commitments, like scouting or sports, saved up all week long, to be released in precious small doses wrapped around a hobby for which the passion still applies. When did we forget that our passion can, and should be what we do? When did play become work for most of us?

Here's an easy question to help you make this relevant. If you won $500,000,000 in the lottery, would you keep the same job that you are in now? Would you? Some people, less that 1% of people whom I have asked this question can say yes. It doesn't matter what job have, what matters if you would do it if you never had to work again a day in your life. That is the job we are now looking for. It's the job you are so good at that you do it nights and weekends, with little or no effort. It's the job that causes you to lose track of yourself, and even lose track of time. It's the perfect job for you, and believe me, it is really out there.

Here's a case in point: I asked someone years ago what they REALLY wanted to be doing with their life. At the time they were selling computer software, and doing fairly well at it. That person said, "Well, when I have $500,000 in the bank I'll be a history teacher for students in 7th and 8th grade." I asked them, "Why don't you do that right now?" and they responded, "I really love teaching, and I love history, but I just can't stand the idea of living now on a teacher's salary"

Seems like a dead end for his dream, doesn't it? Not at all. I suggested that he print up flyers, announcing a trip for 7th and

8th graders to Washington, DC to study history for one week in a group that he would lead, and distribute them in well to do neighborhoods, or run a small ad in a local magazine or newspaper. We did some very quick math and he soon realized that if he could get just 10-12 students at $1500 each that he could earn more than he was making in his current job, and take 9 months off every year! Did he do it? No. Why not? We'll never know, but it illustrates that anything is possible, if you look at it from a new perspective.

When Fred Smith told people that he was going to deliver packages all across the US overnight people told him he was crazy. He did it anyway, and FedEx was born. He followed his passion, his dream, and it worked. Sometimes you have to be a little crazy to get what you want. If you are always blending in, it means you are in the 99% of people, and not in the 1%, but I believe that you are in that 1%. You are a little crazy, and you will live the life of your dreams.

Write down ten things about which you are passionate right now, not ten jobs, but ten anything. Thinking of them puts a smile on your face, and your heart beats a little faster. You wish you go do more of these things, and they may even be your hobbies or a sport that you love. People, places, things, activities, doesn't matter, it's just what you are passionate about right now:

1._____

2._____

3._____

4._____

5._____

6._____

7._____

8._____

9._____

10._____

7. If you could have any job in the world right now, what would it be? Be very specific, what job in what place, and exactly what would you be doing every day?

_____

_____

_____

_____

8. Why?

_____
_____
_____
_____
_____
_____
_____
_____
_____ _____

A friend of mine, Tom Schaff, teaches a seminar on creativity that he begins with a description of babies. He says, "Babies scream a lot, they poop in their pants, spit up, and yet, when someone introduces their new baby to friends, we all say, "Isn't she a miracle?" and, "What a beautiful, wonderful baby?" My friend then asks the question in his seminar, "When did we stop being miracles? When did we lose our dreams, and our passion? When, and more importantly, *why* did we cease to be miracles?

Try right now to think of yourself as a miracle of creation. It is impossible for most of us to fathom, but there was a time when it was true for you, and I believe it still is. I believe that you are not here by chance. None of us are. Of all the billions of people on this earth, literally billions, you are unique. You possess unique gifts and talents that are yours and yours alone, and you can change your future by your will alone. Don't believe it? If you are sitting down right now, stand up! STAND UP, or at least LOOK UP!   Do it!

What started out as a new thought, *I think I'll stand up* ...just happened. It started as your unique thought, and then it happened. Out of the billions of people in the world, you are free to have a new thought, your very own thought, and then make it happen. Wow.

As you consider your unique talents, and the position in life that would ideally suit you best, consider this quote from Marianne Williamson's, *A Return to Love:*

Our deepest fear is not that we are inadequate.
Our deepest fear
is that we are powerful beyond measure.
It is our light, not our darkness,
that most frightens us.
We ask ourselves, who am I
to be brilliant, gorgeous,
talented and fabulous?
Actually, who are you not to be?
You are a child of God.

Your playing small doesn't serve the world.
There is nothing enlightened about shrinking
so that other people won't feel insecure around
you. You are meant to shine, as children do.

We were born to make manifest
the glory of God that is within us.
It's not just in some of us; it's in everyone.
And as we let our own light shine,
we unconsciously give other people
permission to do the same.
As we are liberated from our own fear,
our presence automatically liberates others.

9. Think long and hard about what unique gifts and talents you bring to the world, ask yourself, your spouse and your friends and family what they feel you do best, and then evaluate yourself on what you do, and what you do not do well, and then write down your honest results here. Assessing yourself in this way may bring about some anxiety, but don't pout! The most precious and valuable gift you can give yourself is the power to realize your true potential, and the tools necessary to create wonders with it. Try and define both your strengths and weaknesses simply, such as, *enjoys meeting new people, works well alone, likes details, loves the outdoors, can't remember details, good at math, creative, hardworking, procrastinates,* etc. Go with your first impressions, and try not to over think the basic likes and dislikes, and talents and skills gaps you have:

Your Strengths   Your Potential Weaknesses

_____   _____

_____   _____

_____   _____

_____   _____

_____   _____

_____   _____

_____   _____

_____   _____

_____   _____

_____   _____

_____   _____

Now go back and cross out all your potential weaknesses, because we all have them, and I have learned that when we focus on our strengths, they provide all the ammunition for shooting for the stars that we will ever need. I recently listened to Marcus Buckingham at a conference, and he shared a new perspective on strengths and weaknesses that I really appreciate. He reminded us that we were taught about our weaknesses as our "areas for improvement" meaning where we should spend our time getting better, so that we would be more successful, but he then presented a better idea. "What if," he suggested to 10,000 of us, "we looked at our strengths as our areas for improvement!" How much better would we be if we got even better at those things we are already good at? Doesn't that make more sense? It sure did to me, and I bet it does to you too. Focus on your strengths, and you will realize your full potential.

Now, looking back at what you do well, what you love to do, and what you are ideally suited to do, given your skills and passion, you may be in the right job now, or if you are looking, then maybe you know what specific type of job will be the best one for you. If not, you may need to change jobs or redefine what it is about the job you have that can capture the passion and the desire that you had as a child. If "fireman" was your heartfelt answer in the third grade, and you are an accountant today, than perhaps the thrill of solving an accounting crisis is where you can sense a bit of the passion that you once felt. If there is no place that your passion is inspired by your current occupation, then you already know it is time to set your sights, and set your goals, towards a new career, but either way, it is time to clearly define your goals, and to define success, in your terms.

Write down your perfect job in detail on the next page. It may be the perfect job you defined earlier, but look at that description again, and refine it here according to your strengths.

My Perfect Job

(Consider who, what , when, where and why)

_____
_____
_____
_____
_____
_____
_____
_____
_____
_____
_____
_____
_____
_____

Spend some serious time on this page, because we really DO become what we think about.

Step 1 **2** 3 4 5 6 7 8

Defining Career Success

You have discovered your passion, now what? It is time to take an inventory of where you are, compared to where you want to be. This inventory must include all the areas of your life, because success is not one-dimensional. Success is defined by having all areas of your life working in harmony, and towards a worthy goal. Before you set goals, let's see where you are starting from right now. I suggest looking at the following areas of your life, and writing down where you are at, what is working, and what is not:

1. Physical

_____
_____
_____
_____

2. Spiritual

_____
_____
_____
_____

3. Family

_____
_____
_____
_____

4. Friends

_____
_____
_____
_____

5. Financial/Work

_____
_____
_____
_____

These are not listed in any particular order, but together they define what and who you are right now, and provide a means by which you can see where you are at today, and more importantly, start to think about who you will become.

I have always defined success not as a reflection of where you are today, but rather, by how far you have come, measured from wherever you started. There is another famous definition of success, that has been attributed to Ralph Waldo Emerson, which goes,

"To laugh often and much;

To win the respect of intelligent people and the affection of children;

To earn the appreciation of honest critics and endure the betrayal of false friends;

To appreciate beauty, to find the best in others;

To leave the world a bit better, whether by a healthy child, a garden patch or a redeemed social condition;

To know even one life has breathed easier because you have lived.

This is to have succeeded."

Success truly can be defined in many ways. Here are a few notable quotes on success that have been attributed to some people you might recognize:

"I don't know the key to success, but the key to failure is trying to please everybody." **Bill Cosby**

"Of course there is no formula for success except perhaps an unconditional acceptance of life and what it brings." **Artur Rubinstein**

"You always pass failure on the way to success." **Mickey Rooney**

"A successful individual typically sets his next goal somewhat but not too much above his last achievement. In this way he steadily raises his level of aspiration." **Kurt Lewin**

"To follow, without halt, one aim: There's the secret of success." **Anna Pavlova**

"Eighty percent of success is showing up." **Woody Allen**

"I owe my success to having listened respectfully to the very best advice, and then going away and doing the exact opposite." **G. K. Chesterton**

How do you define success? That is truly the only measure of success that matters. Think back to your passion, and define success in the only terms that matter...yours. Realize that you cannot arrive at a destination without first knowing where that destination is relative to where you are starting your journey. To this end, take an honest inventory of where you are today, and define a destination, your goals, wisely. Too many of us have spent a lifetime climbing the ladder of success, only to realize that it was leaning against the wrong wall. What does success mean to you, and only you?

Write down your own definition of success:

_____

_____

_____

_____

_____

Now lets spend some time reflecting on your definition of success, in light of your passion, and more specifically, at where you see yourself today, right now. Look back at what you wanted to be when you grew up. Look again at your strengths and weaknesses, and what activities fill you with passion, and joy. Ask friends and family what career they could see you ideally successful in, and more importantly, why? Take a good mental inventory, and even an actual written inventory of what all these attributes say about who you are. Really think about these questions, and write down your thoughts here: (if you are not sure what you are thinking, then just start writing ANYTHING, and keep writing until this section is completely full!)

Now we are going to discover a new way to see yourself, your strengths and weaknesses, and better understand who you are. We are going to learn about your *Personality Style.*

Step   1   2   **3**   4   5   6   7   8

Your Personality Style

You may not even be familiar with the term *Personality Style*, but its origins go back thousands of years. In fact, some of the earliest recorded personality styles and personality typing compared human personalities to the 4 elements known at that time: earth, fire, water and air. Is easy to see where someone who would be defined as a person with a *fire* personality style, might be considered hot tempered, or driven to succeed. A person defined by the element water was considered more flexible and easygoing.

You can begin to see how people can be grouped by their individual personality styles. As far back as we know there have generally been four quadrants into which all people have been placed, or categorized. Hippocrates (430-270 BC) developed the four humors, choleric, melancholic, sanguine, and phlegmatic. More modern versions of Personality Styles or Personality Typing, such as Myers Briggs, DiSC or Insights Discovery divide these four types even further into as many as 16 different categories, or even 72 different personality styles. The bottom line is to understand that there are many ways to determine your unique personality style, and going through exercises to learn your own personality style is one of the most important steps you can take to better understand who you are and what makes you tick.

Most of the training that I have done over the years revolves around personality styles, and each time we introduce these principles to new audiences they are amazed at how accurate the results are, and how eager they are to put this new knowledge into practice. You may already be familiar with some terms used to describe personality traits, such as extrovert, introvert, dominant, etc. You may also be familiar with the myriad companies and tests that are used to determine people's personality types and styles, such as Insights Discovery, Inscape Publishing, DISC, The Platinum Rule, Hermann Brain, Profiles International, and Myers Briggs. These sample companies and tests all provide a basic framework by which one can determine one's unique personality type, and some can even generate a 20-30 page report, describing an individual's type, and that person's strengths and weaknesses, based upon the test results. Short of taking one of the tests, our intention here is to give you a basic description of the classic four types, and also help you put yourself into one of the four buckets, to get an introduction into your own personality style, and what it means to you as we continue further into this material.

The basic understanding you will gain here is by no means complete, but it will be enough information for you to both assess more clearly what your type says about you, and also, it will provide a framework into which you can put people you meet, clients, your boss, spouse, and family members into, so that you can better understand where they are all coming from, and what makes them tick as well.

To introduce you to a four personality type model, we will use the following labels to describe four basic personality types: **Thinker, Director, Relater and Talker.**

Now we will arrange the four types into a graph, with four quadrants, shown here:

Thinker	Director
Relater	Talker

As you can start to guess, you will be predominately one of these four types. Some of you will have a primary type, and possibly a secondary type. Let's see where you fit into this graph we have developed, by adding some labels that will further illustrate what the four labels really mean, and where you fit into the graph. We will do this, by first adding four more descriptors at the top, bottom, and right and left sides of the graph. The first two descriptors represent a scale from the left to the right, as shown here:

	Thinker	Director
Introvert		**Extrovert**
	Relater	Talker

What the words "Introvert" and "Extrovert" represent are really your preferences, meaning that in general, you either tend to tell others what to do, you are outgoing, and get your energy from being around other people, which is extroversion, or that you prefer to ask what needs to be done, you get your energy from being alone, and that you like to keep to yourself, which is introversion. Either trait has its merits, and no one trait by itself is any better or any worse, but we all exhibit a preference. On the previous graph, make a mark on the line between introversion and extroversion that best represents where you see yourself as being most comfortable.

As you can see, you have now selected either the right side, or the left side of the graph. In doing so, have excluded two of the four choices as your dominant personality type.

Now let's add another scale on the vertical axis, task versus relationship, shown here:

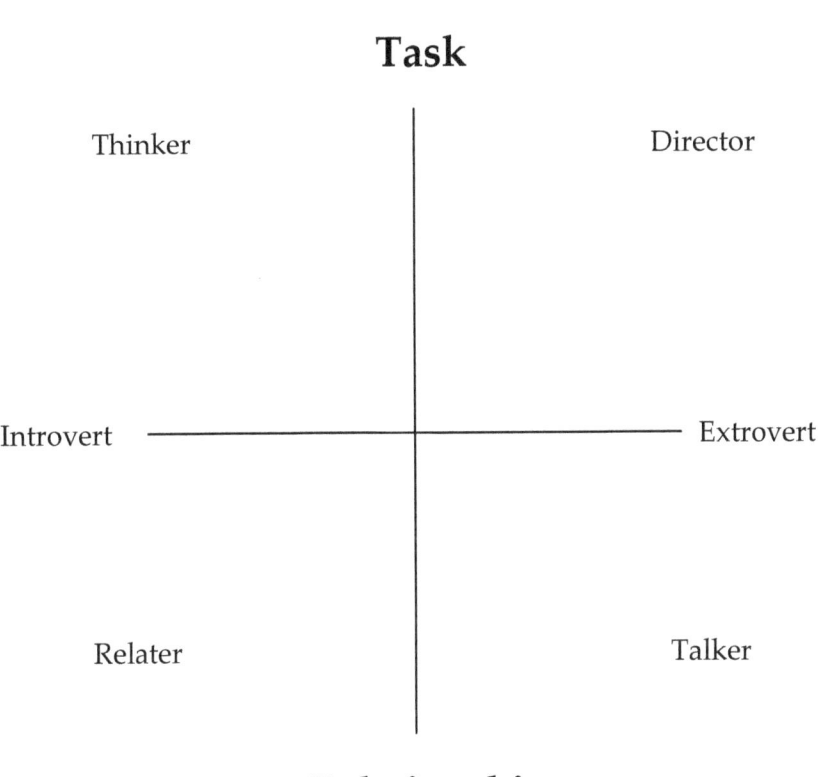

Again, you must choose where to place yourself on this new scale. You either prefer making decisions based upon tasks that

47

need to be completed, and getting things done and accomplished, or you prefer making decisions dealing with people, with their emotions, and with relationships. Make a mark on the vertical line above on the axis which best describes where you are most comfortable.

Now draw 2 lines to connect the two marks that you have make, and where they meet is likely the personality quadrant that describes you best.

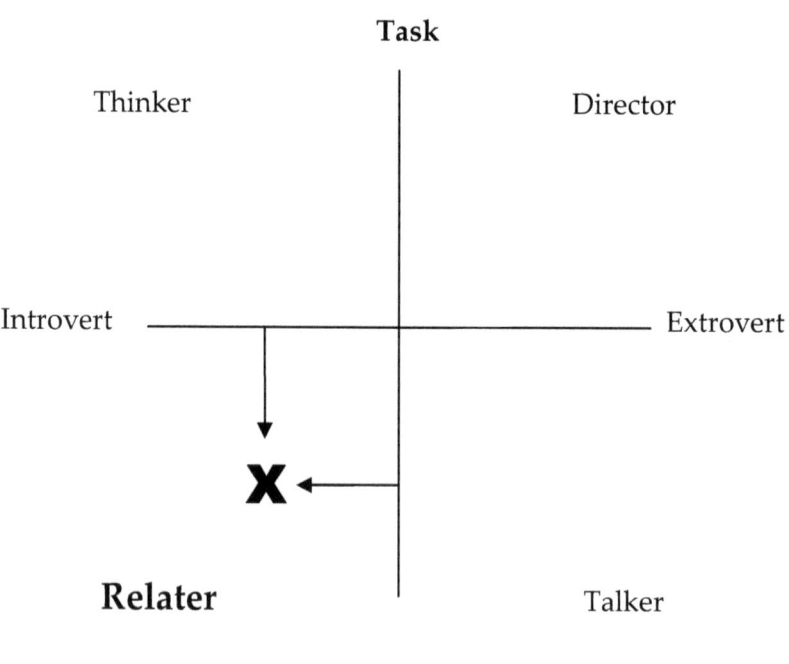

What you have just done, in its most basic form, is placed yourself into only one of the four quadrants. You are now a Director, Relater, Thinker or a Talker. To confirm that this exercise has placed you correctly into the right quadrant, look at the following descriptions of each personality type, and see if in fact it describes you accurately.

Thinker	**Director**
Conscientious	Dominant
Plans ahead	Results Oriented
Careful	Task Focused
Attention to detail	Enjoys a challenge
Relater	**Talker**
Strong inner feelings	Enthusiastic
Works a plan	Life of the party
Prefers little change	Enjoys recognition
Predictable	Talkative

Now, which type are you?

_____

Did you realize that you behave this way? Many people spend their entire lives exhibiting traits like these listed above, without ever realizing that this is the way they are wired, and that they have both strengths, and weaknesses, as a result of which personality type they identify with most. As an example, think of a CEO of a company, who is a Director, which might be a good fit, or how about someone who teaches, a job that a Relater might enjoy very much. Imagine a stand-up comedian; might be a Talker, and an accountant just might be a Thinker.

You can begin to see how your personality type is an excellent data point to consider as you focus in on what work is important to you, and also what you might enjoy doing most. And remember, any personality type can do any job, it just that knowing your own unique style will help you better understand why you like certain roles, and not others. Be open to self-discovery, as all growth, personally and professionally starts with you.

I have taken dozens of personality assessments over the years, and the results are always the same. I am primarily a Talker, and secondly a Director. My wife, Linda is primarily a Director, and secondly a Talker. When we both behave like Directors, we butt heads, as you might imagine, but when we both are behaving like Talkers, we really have a lot of fun together.

Getting to know yourself better is truly a benefit of personality types, and understanding other people's types, based upon their preferences which you observe, is also a benefit. Being able to read other people, and recognize what type they prefer enables you to adapt your style, at times, to better relate to them. An example would be when you, a Talker, are dealing with someone who is doing your taxes, and is likely a Thinker. You would know to hold back some of your exuberance, and stick more to the facts, which in turn, will make your accountant more comfortable dealing with you.

What type is your spouse, partner or significant other?

_____

Name a Thinker, or a Relater that you know:

_____

The greatest Salespeople, and great Managers, have learned to read people all the time, and adapt their particular style at times, to create rapport with people they deal with, and to get more accomplished in less time. Not surprisingly, most of the training I do now centers around teaching people how to understand the four quadrants, and how people can learn who they are, and then accentuate their positives, and minimize their potential weaknesses. Remember what type you are as we move forward in setting goals that are right for you, and take advantage of your particular style. If your personality style was not so easy to determine using this chapter, consider taking an online assessment. The top three I would recommend are:

        Insights Discovery   www.experienceinsights.com

        Myers-Briggs   www.cpp.com

        DiSC   www.inscapepublishing.com

Please consider taking one of the many personality assessments available, to help you better understand your personality style.

Knowing more about how you are wired will help you in your job search and in every other area of your life as well. Additional resources are listed at the back of this book, if you are interested in learning even more about personality style.

Now its time to set down your goals.

Step   1   2   3   **4**   5   6   7   8

Setting Goals

Now it is time to set your goals, select your destination, chart your course, for a definite, and successful future. If you haven't set goals for yourself before, there is an excellent acronym that can help you. The acronym is SMART, and leads you to setting SMART goals.

SMART goals are:

Simple

Measurable

Attainable

Results Oriented

Time Sensitive

Spend time reflecting on your goals, in light of your passion, and where you are at today. Think about your particular personality style, and what you want to accomplish, given who you are, and what you do best.

My Goals

Physical

_____

_____

_____

Spiritual

_____

_____

_____

Family

_____

_____

_____

Friends

_____

_____

_____

Financial/Work

_____

_____

_____

For the last 21 years, since a friend first shared the "secret" of goal setting with me at age 25, I have written down my goals every year, and POSTED them on my bathroom mirror, where I see them, and re-read them every morning and every evening. If you take only one action after reading this guidebook, Please, please, please WRITE DOWN YOUR GOALS and READ THEM EVERYDAY! You too, will succeed, and get the job you want.

As further proof this formula works, here are a few of my goals that I wrote down, and have read everyday for the last ten years. As I write this guidebook, these were all written down, and have all come true:

Be a business leader

Take a year off

Fly fish in Colorado

Take an ocean vacation

Write a book

Fly in a helicopter

Golf in Scotland

Win a golf tournament

As I achieve some of the goals that I have set for myself, I replace them with others:

Fly in a fighter jet

Speak fluent Spanish

Learn sign language

Climb Kilimanjaro

Speak to 10,000 people

Get SCUBA Certified

Visit Tibet

An excellent way for you to post your goals, and track your success everyday is to buy a dry erase marker pen, the kind that are used to write on whiteboards. This is what I use to write my goals down on my bathroom mirror even today, and it is what you can use, too. You can purchase the markers from any office supply store, and I strongly suggest that you do. If you are truly committed to success, then get the markers, and write down your goals on the mirror that you look into each morning, and again each night. This is so simple, but I promise you, less than 10% of the people that purchased this guidebook will do even this much, but that the wealth accumulated by those 10% will be greater than the other 90% combined. Be a success, be in that 10%.

As you start to program your thoughts, there are only two possible outcomes. The universe conspires to turn your goals into reality, or you give up on your goals, and stop posting them, and reading them every day.

Set down this book, and write down your goals right now. If you are not sure what to write, then simply write down, "I will write down my goals this week!" See how easy it is to get started?

Step 1 2 3 4 **5** 6 7 8

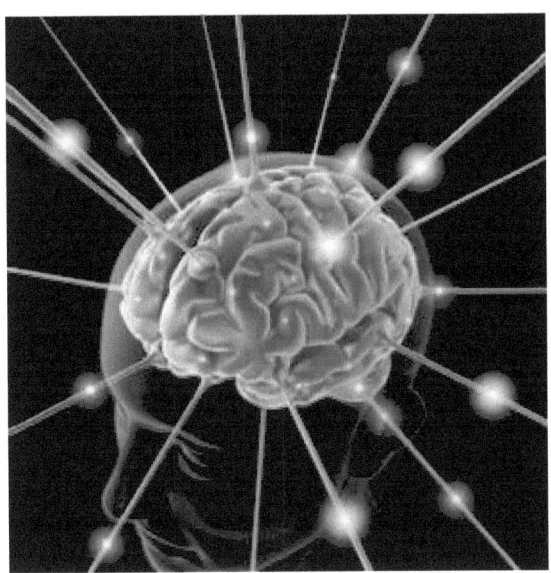

Learning to Think!

There is a famous recording made by Earl Nightingale in 1956, called "The Strangest Secret". A friend gave it to me at age 25, and it changed my life. In fact, I have heard that it is the first talk record to ever become a million seller. It is not as famous today as it once was, but its message is timeless. Mr. Nightingale suggests that even though we all desired at one time to be successful, we simply forgot about it over time. Incredible! We could never forget our goals, our passion, our mission for success, could we? That sad truth is that we can, and most of us have. Still trying to remember what your passion was, and is today? If you haven't thought about it recently, then you have forgotten, and that is the single most important factor in your success, or lack of success, in everything you do.

To begin to really understand this powerful concept, we need to go back to the beginning. For me, this means going back to the bible, where we have all read or heard the phrase, "What ye reap, so shall ye sow". Growing up in a small town in Wisconsin I took this as a child and through my teen years to mean that if someone cleared their fields, planted good seeds, and tended their crops diligently, they would enjoy a bountiful harvest in the fall. What I didn't realize until I was 25 years old was that it means so much more; that this simple phrase holds the key to all the success that I have had in my life, and that it holds the key for your success as well.

Having spent 15 years in the computer business, it is impossible for me not to cite a metaphor that those of you with a personal computer, or access to one will immediately understand. For the rest of you, just stay with me, and I'll bring it all back around. At the heart of every computer is a processor, Intel being probably the most famous. This processor can do no more, and no less than execute the commands that it has received. If the input is good data, or good information, then the processor executes the commands, and returns good data, good information. Simple really, and the same data running through the same computer will return the same results time after time, after time.

Technology folks have summarized this concept in an acronym, "GIGO" which stands for "garbage in, garbage out". Input good data, get good results, input bad data…you get the idea. "GIGO" Remember this, because this is where the metaphor hits home, and unfortunately, this is what most of us are doing unconsciously with our minds all the time, the most powerful computer the world will ever see.

The Power of our Minds

How many of us really think about the power of our minds? Do you ever wonder how much of our mind's power we really use? According to some experts the average person consciously uses less than 10% of the computing power of our minds. I suggest that the crime here is not the amount of our minds that we consciously use, but rather the manner by which use this, our most valuable human asset. What manner is this? It is that we use, we program our minds, most of the time unconsciously! We don't even think about the data, or the information that we are putting into our minds in the first place!

As Earle Nightingale said in his famous recording from 1956, "The reason men [and women] are not successful is because they don't THINK! Sure we all go through the motions everyday, in all our actions and all out routines, but how often do we consciously THINK? How often do we CONCIOUSLY select good input to put into our minds, so that after our minds process the information, we get good, and <u>predetermined</u> results. The results that we are really after in the first place, like having a happy marriage, being a good father, or having a successful and rewarding career.

How often do you select the proper input to achieve the desired results that you seek? Not sure how to do this? Intrigued? Read on.

Programming your Mind

Just like in the computer metaphor, our minds are at idle, until we give them input to process. We provide this input with what we see, what we hear, what we feel, touch and even taste. Our senses are the only external ways we can define the input, and they shape our thoughts and determine our future. Did you realize there is a much more important means by which we deliver input into our minds? It is through the questions that we ask of ourselves, consciously, subconsciously and even unconsciously.

These inputs are the real and very, very powerful programs that we unleash to run in our minds, and they are running every second of every minute of every day. When the questions are conscious, we often times are not even aware that we are setting these negative programs into motion. It happens when we say to ourselves, "How come I never get a break" or " How come I am so unlucky?" These types of questions, once asked of ourselves, set the world's most powerful computer into motion, trying to resolve the questions, the programs, that we have selected to run, and the power, and the horror, is that once set into motion, these programs use every possible input that they can find to answer the questions we have asked.

Here are a few examples: If we have asked of ourselves, "How come I never get a break", then our minds will seek out and validate every input that satisfies the question. Our minds will offer up answers, or output like, "The reason I never get a break is that life is unfair, and I will always end up with the short end of the stick" or when we ask ourselves, " Why am I in a dead end job?" our minds will find examples to support our questions, and answer us, " You are in a dead end job because you couldn't get a better job even if you tried" Get it? Are you starting to see how we can influence, and be influenced by what we think about. The message I am sharing with you is that we truly do become what we think about. What do you think about?

What questions do you ask yourself everyday? Are they thoughtful, careful questions, like, " How can I do more at work to get a raise?" and " What can I do today to be a better father?" or are they thoughts like, " Why am I in such a dead end job?" and "Why are people always such a pain?" Ask, and you shall receive. What are you asking for? Do you know?

If you really did just write down your goals, then you are in the 1% of people who really KNOW!

Now let's see how we learn best.

Visual, Auditory and Kinesthetic Learners

As I mentioned earlier, input into our minds is received through our 5 physical senses, and also through a more difficult to understand, "sixth sense" often referred to as intuition. Of these, taste and smell are not statistically significant for us to discuss here, unless your goal is to be a professional chef, and intuition is very difficult to quantify, and hard for many people to understand. Some people believe that intuition represents "the universe" or "energy" or spirituality, while others argue that there is no such thing. For Carl Jung, it is our ancestors speaking to us through the collective unconscious. For me, intuition, or *knowing* something, is based in my belief in God. If any one of these works for you, then use it, if it doesn't, then intuition may not be a tool that you can, or want to rely upon. It begs far more time for discussion than we have here, but keep it in the back of your mind. We are primarily concerned here with the three main senses we use most of the time to receive input into our minds, and which will be defined more clearly here; namely, our sense of sight, (visual) hearing, (auditory) and touch, (kinesthetic).

Our sight, or visual input dominates most of what we all bring into our minds everyday. It has been shown that our minds can process visual information that it receives ten times faster than when we hear it, but that our retention tends to be higher when we receive input through our ears. Additionally, some people favor their kinesthetic sense, or their sense of touch. Regardless of which of these three senses you favor most, it is important to be aware that we are in control of what we take in through these senses. If we are primarily visual, then what we CHOOSE to look at determines what we see. If we are primarily auditory, then what we CHOOSE to listen to determines what we hear. If we are primarily kinesthetic, then what we CHOOSE to do determines what we experience.

What input are you CHOOSING each day? Is it a conscious decision? It should be, and especially when you look at, (or hear, or experience) your goals, then you are putting the right thoughts in motion, which will inevitably lead to the predetermined results you seek.

Once you accept and believe that your mind operates in this manner, you will always set the right programs into motion to get what you want. This is the key to success. We all do become what we think about. The problem is not that we are all choosing to program failure and unhappiness into our minds, and into our lives, but that rather that we are not consciously programming success into our minds and into our lives.

Sadly, most of us are all operating on autopilot, and the inputs that we are programming into our minds, from the traffic jam on the way to work, to the depressing morning news we watched, to the grumbling and destructive questions we are asking ourselves after skipping breakfast and rushing out the door, late for work almost without realizing that we are doing so, are the wrong programs that then run ALL DAY in our minds until we CHOOSE to input new programs, and ask ourselves new questions. If you haven't thought about what questions you are asking yourself, and about what inputs you are receiving from other people, television, radio, etc. then you are going nowhere at best, and at worst, you are quietly on a negative path of destruction, blaming others for results that you simply forgot to control, and to determine in advance, based upon your passion, and the goals that you have set for yourself. A sad truth that I have heard in the past is that most of us spend more time planning a weekend vacation, than we do planning for the rest of our lives, and our careers. Is this true for you?

How exciting that we can change this at anytime, by following through with the five steps described here so far, and, assuming you have defined goals as a result of what you have read and learned so far, you are on your way to the front of the pack, the top of the mountain of success, where, If I may paraphrase what Earle Nightingale said in his audio book *Lead the Field*, "When you are on top, the sun rises earlier, sets later, the people are nicer, they smile a lot more,…its nicer up here."

Let's look at how fundamental this programming principle is to all of us. What were your waking thoughts this morning? Were they in alignment with your goals; were they negative, or just neutral? You probably can't even remember, and therefore your subconscious mind, the infinitely powerful part of your mind, that could have been seeking out opportunities throughout the day, to aid you in the completion of your goals, ran on autopilot, AND IN THE WRONG DIRECTION! Let's fix that starting tomorrow, and for the rest of your successful life.

Tonight, write yourself a positive note, an affirmation, such as, "Today I will see the best in other people, whether they cut me off on my drive into work, (maybe they are having a personal crisis, and they need to get into work or they will lose their job, etc) or whether they are my coworkers, and I will compliment them when I can" Write down your own affirmation tonight, and set it on your alarm clock, or using a dry erase pen, write it on your bathroom mirror. If you have already written down your goals as suggested earlier, then use them. Now, as you awake tomorrow, read it before you are even fully awake, and you will have taken the first true step towards controlling your thoughts, and therefore controlling your future.

If you want to really leverage your sensory inputs, and you should, then read your goals aloud, and feel the excitement that reading them generates. This will enable you to engage all your primary senses to help you realize your goals. DO NOT wake up, turn on the television, or the radio, and listen to all the naysayers describe all the crime, moral decay and financial hardships the you will surely face throughout the day, instead, control the input you receive, and the outcomes you seek will surely follow, as surely as any computer will output the same results, given the same input. Realize too, that your mind, through your five senses, seeks and receives input all day, starting with your waking thoughts, and will return output, in the form of your thoughts and actions, regardless of what you do, so take control now!

There is clearly a set formula for career success, and getting a job fast. You have learned the first 5 steps of that process so far, and there only 3 more to go!

The first 5 steps that you have learned so far are:

        Find your passion

        Define career success

        Know your personality style

        Set your goals

        Learn to Think!

The final three steps, which are no less important than the first 5 are:

        Operate with Integrity

        Execute Daily

        Giving Back

These five principles are the first half of the formula for success, used by nearly every happy and successful person I have ever met, and it is the surest way for you to become your best, reach your potential, and truly be successful. At this point I really hope you have written in this book. If you did not, your life will not change, and you may not get the job you are seeking. If however, you HAVE written down your answers honestly to these questions, you are in the top 10%. You are a superstar. You will succeed.

Now let's tackle the last three steps of the Get a Job Fast formula.

Step 1 2 3 4 5 **6** 7 8

Operate With Integrity

In the early 1900s, a lot was written about success. The industrial age enabled the likes of Andrew Carnegie and Henry

Ford to rise as business leaders, and their lives, and their extraordinary success became the subject of many writings and studies. One theme that runs throughout these writings is the character of these successful men, and others from that era. Integrity emerged as one trait that all these men shared, and integrity was credited as a key factor in their success, time and time again. Sadly, in the years from then until now, integrity and character have slid into the shadows, and yet, all the truly successful people that I know have these traits top on their list. I know people, too, that are financially successful, but they are not men and women of character, and their lives are disconnected. Success must be the definition of a whole person, whose goals, actions thoughts and character are in place, complete, and worthy of exemplification. A person can only lead a life of integrity if both their personal life, and their business life reflect the same integrity.

In the wake of political marital infidelity and questionable financial deals on Wall Street, and with political heroes placed on a pedestal for their professional lives, while they cheat on their wives and their taxes, the media has created the illusion for so many people today that success can be achieved in the absence of integrity. It cannot. The quality of your character will determine your degree of professional and personal success. The two cannot be separated.

I will never forget, as a child of about 10 years old, cleaning my father's law office on the weekends to earn a few extra bucks. He came in one weekend while I was working, and made a few phone calls. I saw him make the calls, then write down notes, and put a number beside each note, like .25, or .50. I asked him what the numbers meant, and he shared that it was how he billed his clients, that .25 was a quarter hour, and .50 a half hour of his time. I remember asking him, "Why don't you just write down a bigger number, and charge them more for your work?" He told me that people did business with him because of his integrity, and that if he let it slip, even a little bit, that he would never be able to gain it back. That message has stuck with me all this time. It is often much harder to do the right thing, but the rewards are long-term, and this is what I mean by integrity. We have all heard the phrase, "What goes around, comes around" and nowhere does this ring true as much as it pertains to character. Decide now to make your character exceptional, and the success, and self-confidence that you seek will be yours.

While integrity can define how we conduct ourselves, it can also be used to define the environments we choose to spend our personal and professional time in. I saw Lance Secretan speak ten years ago, he had written a successful book titled, *Reclaiming Higher Ground,* that I highly recommend. In his speech to us at the annual conference for Computer Training Companies, he shared a few examples of integrity displayed by corporations. One example was the 2% milk that many of us used to purchase and consume everyday. He asked a room of about 400 people what the percentage of fat there was in whole milk. Most of the room raised their hands for 100%. Lance then shared with us that whole milk is only about 4%, and that 2% milk is a misleading indicator of the difference between the two products. It is legal, but is it moral?

A second example that hit home with me was about a jar of spaghetti sauce, labeled "fresh tasting" rather than fresh, because it was really not fresh, but that corporation somehow had its corporate lawyers fight for the right to use the phrase, "fresh tasting." Legal, yes, but moral? How about cigarette companies?

Are you looking to work for a company that you are proud of? Make sure integrity defines not just what you do, but where you do it, and with whom.

I recently attended a leadership training session taught by Bill George, the former CEO of Medtronic, sponsored by Tergar Meditation Center, and the University of Minnesota Center for Spirituality and Healing. Spending two days with him was inspiring to me, because he put such great emphasis on integrity, and doing the right thing when it matters most, which is when we are alone. Such a refreshing message, and one which his books, *Authentic Leadership*, and *True North*, define and clarify so well. Make integrity a cornerstone of your life, and spend your life with others who do the same.

Step   1   2   3   4   5   6   **7**   8

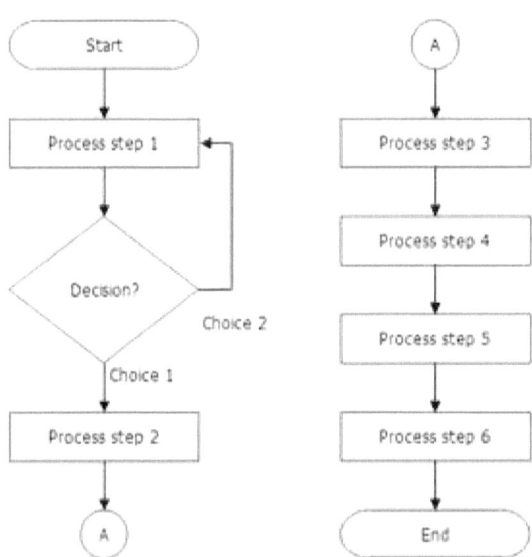

Basic Flowchart

Execution

No guidebook to career success and getting the right job could ever be complete without a commentary on execution. That is, the mean by which we accomplish all that we set out to do. Defining goals based upon your passion, thinking about them, and operating with integrity will not lead to any sustainable amount of success, unless you are committed to staying the course, and EXECUTING on your plans for the attainment of your goals. For some people, success, and financial rewards have come too soon, and without the monotonous daily rigors of execution. Easily won riches will be easily lost, but hard earned wages are your ticket to lasting success.

Let's take some time and define the plans you will use to secure the attainment of the goals that you have defined earlier in this guidebook.

What are the key components of the plan that you will need to execute, in order to achieve the goals that you have defined for yourself? Write down now what you will need to do, and how often, to achieve the goals that you have set for yourself:

How I will EXECUTE to achieve my Goals

Physical

_____

_____

_____

_____

Spiritual

_____

_____

_____

_____

Family

_____

_____

_____

_____

Friends

_____

_____

_____

_____

Financial/Work

_____

_____

_____

_____

Now let's expand this last section, Financial/work, in greater detail. Here are a few more questions that will make the difference in your job search:

What job, at which company, and in what industry?

How will you research your choices?

How will you market yourself?

How will you network with others?

Who will support you?

What job boards, newspapers, and web sites will you read regularly?

What career seminars will you attend?

What motivational tapes and CDs will you listen to?

What additional books will you read?

How many new contacts will you make each day?

Are you on www.LinkedIn.com?

Are you on www.Facebook.com?

Does www.Craigslist.com have your perfect job listed?

What trade Associations could you join?

Can you call the company President directly?

How many contacts can you find through your friends?

Are there state and Federal jobs available?

What government programs can you access?

Can your church, synagogue or temple help you succeed?

Are you committed to doing what it takes to succeed?

I could add five or fifty-five more blank pages here, but it is easier to direct you to www.GetaJobFast.com to see the full list of questions that you must be able to answer. It is really up to you to define your plans, at whatever level of detail it takes for you to succeed.   If creating the plan necessary to achieve your goals is difficult, or you need help, email me your goals at scott@getajobfast.com, and I'll offer any assistance that I can to help you define what you need to do to succeed. Do not continue reading until you have answered at least a few of the previous questions. Your future depends on it!

Believe it or not, defining one's plan is not the area where most of us fail, but rather in not defining WHAT we are setting out to do, or not having the motivation to pursue the goals that we have set for ourselves. Where there is a will, there is a way. Have you ever heard this phrase before? Do not lose heart if defining your plan is more difficult that you thought it would be, keep looking back at your goals, stay in touch with your passion, and realize that you will find a way. Thomas Edison, upon documenting that his 10,000 attempt at identifying the right filament for inside his soon to be perfected incandescent bulb, did not work, was reportedly asked how it felt to fail 10,000 times, to which Mr. Edison reportedly answered, "I have not failed, I have successfully eliminated 10,000 filaments which do not work!" This attitude about failure, simply restated as, failure is only one of the necessary elements that leads so many to their eventual success, is a badge of honor that all the successful entrepreneurs that I know wear with pride.

Another aspect of your plan, and the execution of it, is to realize that even before the ink is dry, (even as it rolls off your printer), that it will be obsolete almost immediately. People change, circumstances change, but what rarely changes is our passions, and if we have defined our goals thoughtfully and in light of our passions, then they will remain consistent also. They serve as the lighthouse that will direct us steadfast towards goals that we are passionate about. The purpose of a plan of execution is to serve as a roadmap, which we understand will change over time. It serves as a guidepost to show us how we are doing in our quest towards our goals. Stay the course and you will succeed.

The hardest aspect of the execution of your plan (remembering that execution itself is not the hardest part of your success formula, but that rather defining what you want, and why is really where most people fail) is to do what needs to be done, when it needs to be done, towards the completion of your goals. A great question I often ask myself as I look on my own plans, especially at times of weakness, is "If I look back an hour from now, what actions should I take that will leave me the most satisfied AFTER THE ACTION HAS BEEN COMPLETED?" I don't mean to pretend that I always take the right actions afterwards, but I ALWAYS know which action I <u>should</u> have chosen.

Another way to say this to yourself, is, "What would the person that I plan to become do right now?" Print both these questions on a postcard, and carry them with you, because even around the area of execution, what matters most is to Think! Think about why you are choosing to execute your plan, what about the plan drives you towards your passion, and how good it feels to succeed. Look to the lighthouse that is your goals, to help you through the tough times.

Weight loss is a great example of where these questions or another phrase that I have heard fits into our day-to-day, decision-making process. The phrase is, "Nothing tastes as good as being thin feels." (Try it when you're hungry.) Successful execution of our plans towards our goals is an everyday, all the time thing. We will all fail at times to stay the course, but success is achieved when we get back up after we have fallen, when we get back on the horse that threw us, when we jump back on the bicycle and keep riding. A Chinese proverb simply states, "fall down seven times, get up eight"

What enables us to do this is the endgame. It is our lighthouse. Our GOALS, fueled with the all the passion that we have been able to muster as we defined them, and read them every morning and again every evening, and consume them through our senses every day.

Thinking daily about your goals is the surest way to sustain yourself, especially when executing the plan is hard. No one achieves lasting success without getting through the tough spots. If you have defined the right goals which you are passionate about, then you have all the ammunition you will ever need to keep you going, through all the difficulties that you encounter. Remember, anything worth getting is worth fighting for. Are you willing to fight to achieve your goals? If so, then you will succeed.

Step   1   2   3   4   5   6   7   **8**

Giving Back

Let's jump ahead in your life one year. You have made significant progress towards your stated goals. In fact, you have even achieved a few of them, and also added a few more. You have a new job that you love, and whose mission and values matches your own. You are physically fit, and proud of the person whom you have become. You wake up passionately every day, re-read your goals, and enter your day pursuing those worthy goals through your intentional and passionate thoughts and actions. You have plans for execution in place that help steer you in the right direction, you are on top, secure in the knowledge that you have unlocked the secret to success, and carry yourself with more self-confidence than you ever thought possible.

Now what?

Now is just the beginning. Now is when it starts to get really fun, because now it you have put yourself in a position to give back. Give back your time, your talents, your joy, your money, you. It is time to give back that part of you that matters to others.

One of the ways that I have always enjoyed giving back is to share books. As I have read books throughout my life, I have given away thousands of them to people that I knew would benefit. In fact, I founded the web site www.selfconfidence.com in 1996 simply because I was couldn't keep up buying certain books one or two at a time to give to other people whom I would meet often while traveling, so I set up the site to allow people to jump online and learn key concepts about success there, and also order the books themselves. I get great joy out of hearing back from someone that a book or tape that I gave them helped them achieve their goals, and I have realized, as many of us do, as we grow older, that there is much greater satisfaction in helping others, than there is in helping ourselves. The catch is, to really be able to help other people; we need to have at least operated our own lives in a way that sustains our ability to give back, whether it is our time, our talents or our other resources. Hopefully, your new understanding of the principles of success will put you well on your way to being able to give back, more than you ever thought you could.

What will you give back to the world? When? It should be a key part of your personal plan for success. Even if you are struggling as you work through this document, whether financially, or searching for deeper meaning in your life, you are able to begin giving back right now, whether through a smile to the check out clerk, letting the obnoxious driver that is intent on cutting you off merge in front of you, or even providing more warmth for your spouse and your family.

Opportunities to give back exists every day, and the more we take advantage of them, the more we are affirmed that we really do control our own destiny, and that although we cannot control the circumstances around us, what we can always control our response to those circumstances, and our surroundings.

We are all responsible, meaning, that we are all

response able,

We are able to **choose our response**, at any time, to whatever happens to us.

Never again say "I have to…" or " I need to…" instead teach yourself to say "I choose to…" in every circumstance, because it is TRUE! Everything that happens in our lives that we do, we chose to do. This single most fundamental concept will change the way you look at every aspect of your life. Start saying "I choose to…" today. Reinforce the concept that you really are in charge of your destiny.

When I grew up, my parents had a plaque on the wall in our hallway, which I read everyday, but for which the significance did not hit me until I was about 30 years old. Its author is anonymous, and I have heard it described as "The Serenity Prayer".

God, grant me the serenity

To accept the things

That I cannot change,

The courage to change

The things that I can, and

The wisdom

To know

The difference.

I never gave much thought to this prayer as I grew up, but seeing it everyday burned it into my subconscious, so that when I discovered its meaning later in life, I think of it all the time. Its real meaning to me is:

God, grant me the serenity

To accept

WHAT HAPPENS TO ME!

The courage to change

HOW I RESPOND! And

The wisdom

To know

The difference.

I suggest that you find a phrase, poem or prayer that reminds you that we are all in charge of our destiny, that we are always able to choose how we respond in any given situation, and that those of who count ourselves among life's successful, are living a life on purpose, moving in the direction of worthy goals, and able to give back to others at any time, for the sole purpose of helping others and helping better the world. Post it on your mirror, put a copy in your car, and at your office, and even on your refrigerator.

Earl Nightingale said 50 years ago, "**We become what we think about**"

It is written in the Bible, "**As a man thinketh in his heart, so is he**"

Even Buddha said, "**What we think, we become**"

What are you waiting for?

Steps 1 2 3 4 5 6 7 8

Conclusion

There is a formula for job success, and it has now been shared with you in eight steps. You now know that you are responsible for your own personal degree of happiness, success and self-confidence, and you can no longer blame others. Each day, when you look in the mirror, be sure to smile at the person that can make all your dreams come true, and when necessary, review the 8 steps summarized again for you here:

Step 1. Find Your Passion – What would you do if you had all the money, and all the time in the world? What parts of your job and your life are consistent with your passion?

Step 2. Define Career Success – In the only terms that matter, yours.

Step 3. Know your Personality Style - Use this knowledge to achieve your goals, and take an assessment to learn more.

Step 4. Set Goals – Set SMART goals around every area of your life, and write them down. Read them every morning, and again at night.

>Physical
>
>Spiritual
>
>Family
>
>Friends
>
>Financial/Work

Step 5. Think! - Post your goals, and read them daily, to define your thoughts, which will shape your daily actions, which will lead you inevitably to your successful future. Use the unlimited power of your mind.

Step 6. Operate with Integrity – Operate your life, that is, your personal and your professional life, because they cannot be separated, just as you cannot live these two aspects of your life separately, in a way the exemplifies a man or woman of character. Be of the highest character in all your endeavors, and with whom you spend your time.

Step 7. Execute – Clearly write down a plan that helps you move towards your goals. Remember that your passion and goals will sustain you through the hard times, but never give up, never quit.

Step 8. Give back – Success when measured by what you alone achieve will never sustain you long term. Start now giving out a smile when you can, a helping hand, and realize you are planting the seeds of giving in your life that will enable you to look back on a long life, and feel it was well lived. God bless you in your journey, I wish you all the success in the world, and if I can aid you in the completion of your goals, then email them to me at scott@getajobfast.com, and lets arrive at your final, successful destination together.

Scott Schwefel

About the author:

Scott Schwefel was raised in Beaver Dam, Wisconsin, by parents that taught him the value of finding one's passion, goal setting, hard work, integrity and the need to give back. He attended the University of Minnesota, for engineering, and later received his degree from Concordia University in Organizational Development and Communications. He launched several startup companies in his early twenties, and also sold computers to pay the rent each month. In 1989 he and his partners raised nearly a million dollars in venture capital, and built and sold a multimillion dollar food company. He married his wife Linda in 1989, and together they began teaching, writing and defining the principles in this guidebook, by launching a sales training company in 1991.

In 1995 Mr. Schwefel founded Benchmark Learning, which he grew to become Minnesota's largest technology training center. During this time, he interviewed more than 500 job candidates, and realized that there were a small number of people who although in a job search, were totally in control of their destiny, and it showed. He began to understand why these job candidates were different from the others, and how they understood the principles in this book. After a transformative month living with the Massai and Hadza tribes in Tanzania, Africa, he returned home, sold his interest in Benchmark for more than a million dollars to take a year off and write this book on the principles of success that helped him personally succeed.

Scott Schwefel and his wife Linda make their home in Excelsior, Minnesota, with their 3 children, McKenzie, Connor and Scottie Nicole.

Scott is available for speaking, training and coaching engagements on any of the principles contained in this guidebook. He enjoys delivering keynotes to thousands, conducting small group workshops, or one on one mentoring of CEOs and Executives.

Email scott@getajobfast.com, contact the Scott at 952-223-1147, or visit www.scottschwefel.com to learn more.

Scott Schwefel

684 Excelsior Blvd.

Suite 100

Excelsior, MN 55331

Additional recommended reading, or audio book selections, by the author:

The Strangest Secret by Earl Nightingale

The Psychology of Achievement by Brian Tracy

The Psychology of Selling by Brian Tracy

Repacking Your Bags by Richard Leider

Lead the Field by Earl Nightingale

How to Win Friends and Influence People by Dale Carnegie

Think and Grow Rich by Napolean Hill

Do What You Love, The Money Will Follow by Marsha Sinetar

The E-Myth by Michael Gerber

Authentic Leadership by Bill George

True North by Bill George

More reading suggestions, and additional free resources are at www.GetaJobFast.com

This book is available for quantity purchase at significant discounts for colleges, universities, placement firms, churches, government agencies, job boards, resume writers, search firms, and recruiting companies. This final page can also be customized with your message in conjunction with any purchase over 100 copies.

Please contact us to learn more. scott@getajobfast.com, www.getajobfast.com, or call 952-454-4065 for rates on quantity discounts.

www.ingramcontent.com/pod-product-compliance
Ingram Content Group UK Ltd.
Pitfield, Milton Keynes, MK11 3LW, UK
UKHW041958230426
12048UKWH00008B/400